MOTIVATING YOUR TRAINEES

101
Proven Ways to
Get Them to
Really Want
to Learn

■ ■ ■

By Bob Pike with Randy Johnson

Lakewood Publications
A Maclean Hunter Company

Quantity Sales

Most Lakewood books are available at special quantity discounts when purchased in bulk by companies, organizations and special-interest groups. Custom imprinting or excerpting can also be done to fit special needs. For details contact Lakewood Books.

■ ■ ■

LAKEWOOD BOOKS

50 South Ninth Street
Minneapolis, MN 55402
(800) 707-7769 or (612) 333-0471
FAX (612) 340-4819

Publisher: Philip G. Jones
Editors: Bob Pike with Julie Tilka
Production Editor: Julie Tilka
Production: Carol Swanson and Pat Grawert
Cover Designer: Barb Betz, Betz Design

10 9 8 7 6 5 4 3 2 1

Lakewood Publications, Inc. publishes *TRAINING Magazine; Training Directors' Forum Newsletter; Creative Training Techniques Newsletter; Technology For Learning Newsletter; Potentials In Marketing* Magazine, *Presentations* Magazine; and other business periodicals, books, research and conferences.

Bob Pike, Creative Training Techniques International, 7620 W. 78th St., Edina, MN 55439, (612) 829-1960, FAX (612) 829-0260.

ISBN 0-943210-68-2

Contents

Foreword

This book, *Motivating Your Trainees*, is one in a series drawn from the best content of *Creative Training Techniques Newsletter*. The newsletter was conceived in 1988 by editor and internationally known trainer Bob Pike to be a one-stop resource of practical "how-tos" for trainers. The idea was (and still is) to provide timely tips, techniques, and strategies that help trainers with the special tasks they perform daily.

When the newsletter began, it was largely fueled by Bob's 20 years of experience in the field and by the best ideas shared by the trainers (more than 50,000 in all) who had attended his Creative Training Techniques seminars. As the newsletter grew in popularity, it also began to draw on ideas submitted by its readers. Today, the newsletter continues to search out creative approaches from the more than 200 seminars Bob and the other Creative Training Techniques trainers conduct every year, and from the newsletter readers.

But no matter where the insights come from, the goal of the newsletter remains the same: To provide trainers a cafeteria of ideas they can quickly absorb, and then choose those that best suit their special needs.

This series of books represents the best ideas from *Creative Training Techniques Newsletter's* six years of publication. It is our hope we've created a valuable resource you'll come back to again and again to help address the unique challenges you face in your job every day.

Sincerely,
The Editors

Introduction

Motivating learners can be one of your greatest challenges as a professional trainer. You can't teach people who don't see a reason to learn what you're offering. What you can do, however, is create an environment that invites trainees to motivate themselves, by keeping your approach to training them fresh and exciting.

Motivating Your Trainees contains the best ideas from the first six years of *Creative Training Techniques Newsletter* for keeping your delivery inviting and accessible, and for preparing your participants to gain the most from training. The tips in this book range from simple ways to rouse drowsy students to unique approaches to engage trainees in role-plays to creative ways to help trainees use their newfound knowledge back on the job.

The book is divided into two sections. The first section, *Delivery Tips*, focuses on things you can do to add flavor and flair to your presentations in ways that not only enhance the "listenability" of sessions, but improve their content as well. Tips include games, methods for emphasizing key points, simple ways to make your message more meaningful, and more. The second section, *Learner Motivation Techniques*, focuses on ways trainers can encourage participants to *want* to learn — and to use the knowledge they gain as a valuable resource back on the job.

Every idea is classroom-tested by people just like you — professional trainers. These techniques are proven methods for dealing with situations you've quite likely encountered and will encounter again. Read them —

then modify, adjust, and adapt them to meet your needs. You may even want to make this book a part of your training tool kit. Carry it with you to consult for quick, creative ways to customize your training to meet new situations as they arise.

Treat this book as a smorgasbord. You dont' have to eat everything offered to have a great meal. And you can always come back for seconds. Bon appetit!

Bob Pike

Section One: Delivery Tips

Getting across your learning points is the biggest challenge faced when making a presentation. Some of the most important basic guidelines include:

• *Present single ideas.* Many members of any audience will quickly get lost if you throw too many ideas at them at once. Encourage participants to react to an idea once you've presented it. Also, ask people to "buy off" on an idea before presenting another.

• *Be as specific as possible.* Avoid generalizations.

• *Follow a logical sequence.* Put your ideas in a sequence that makes sense to your listeners, either chronological, topical, or from least to most important words.

• *Use a language common to your listeners.* Avoid jargon and unfamiliar terms or words.

• *Know your purpose.* Ask yourself, "What is my goal in communicating this information?"

• *Give your audience an overview.* Remember the axiom: "Tell them what you're going to tell them, tell them, then tell them what you told them." Lay the foundation for the material you'll cover. Define key terms. Build a common ground with your audience.

1

Guidelines ensure the audience gets your learning points

2

No training need be boring — no matter how dull the content

Who says dull material has to be dull? If you're dealing with material labeled dry or boring, ask two questions: "Who says it's boring?" You? The participants? Past participants? Second, ask, "Why is it boring?" Is is the content? The fact that participants are required to attend? How it's been presented in the past? The instructor's style?

The answers to these two questions can help you identify the problems you have to confront, and which of the following suggestions might help.

1. *Help participants see the relevance of the material.* Use a case study to introduce the material and put it into a "real world" context.

2. *Help participants see a personal payoff.* Use the two questions, "What kinds of problems have you seen people get into when they don't...?" and "What kinds of problems have you seen trainers have because they don't involve their participants?" Or, "What happens when you and I do involve our participants?" By personalizing the once-boring material you help participants see benefits to gain and losses to avoid in applying the content of the course.

3. *Have participants develop case*

studies or problems that can be passed on to other participants in the group. Look at television game shows to identify formats or approaches. For example, a "Family Feud" approach might work if you wanted to make people aware of:

• Common causes of customer complaints.

• Most common mistakes in repairing equipment.

• What employees want most in a work environment.

3

Unseen expert grabs trainees' attention

Holding a conversation with "the voice" of some unseen entity is a sure way to get the attention of a class, according to Val Larson, training supervisor for Borg-Warner.

Larson plays an audiotape through the classroom public address system and converses with the voice — addressing her comments toward the ceiling — about topics related to the training program. She says the method never fails to gain the attention of her participants.

Tom Cunningham, training supervisor for William Brown Publishers, expects new sales representatives to take six to 12 months to get up to speed with product knowledge, techniques, and paperwork they must master.

At the initial training session for new representatives, Cunningham says, newcomers frequently feel intimidated when they meet representatives with three or more years experience.

Cunningham addresses this problem by including a sales representative on his training team with just one year of experience — someone who was in the new trainees' shoes the previous year. When Cunningham reveals during the training session that a rookie is in their midst, it helps the new representatives realize that they, too, will be able to assimilate all the material within a year.

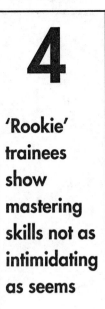

4

'Rookie' trainees show mastering skills not as intimidating as seems

5

Trainees prove to themselves that bad news travels fast

With so many companies turning their attention to customer satisfaction, one of the first messages new employees often receive is about the role each person plays in providing good service.

To help make the point, Ellen Edwards, director of education for Rush Health Plans, asks attendees during one segment of her orientation program to act as experts (experienced customers) and think of experiences they've had with good and bad customer service.

Participants are usually more eager to talk about bad service they've experienced. After the group has shared its experiences, Edwards points out that spreading the bad news is common; indicative of often-cited studies that show most dissatisfied customers do not complain to the company; they quietly take their business elsewhere, and then typically tell at least 10 people about their bad service experience.

The point is made even more clear to her participants because they have just revealed that very data themselves.

6

Using acronyms helps trainees remember concepts

Acronyms are a good review tool when used to help participants remember concepts that are used repeatedly, says Maria Rael, implementation consultant for Delphi Information Systems. For instance, her trainees must specify on their computer screens, whether to **A**dd, **D**elete, **M**odify, **I**nquire, or **T**erminate. The choices are easily remembered with the word **ADMIT**.

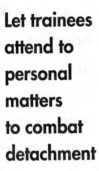

7

Let trainees attend to personal matters to combat detachment

Preoccupation can be a major barrier to learning. To keep trainees from becoming detached during his three-week technical courses, Stewart Alred, technical trainer for Maryland Casualty, selects a block of time in the middle of one day in the second week of the course to allow trainees to attend to personal matters.

Alred allows from 10 a.m. to 2 p.m. for trainees to meet with their mentors or relocation coordinators. This allows the trainees to keep focused on training during class time, especially during vital third week activities which require the most concentration.

Room arrangement can be critical to getting training results, says Andrea Tinkham, human services program specialist for the Florida Department of Health and Rehabilitative Services.

In computer training, for example, Tinkham finds it useful to train from the *back* of the room if computers are set up in the center of the classroom, or to move the computers near the walls so she can circulate in the center of the room to monitor the progress of the group.

8

Strategic seating gets training results

9

Kids' blocks are multipurpose visual aids

Lego building blocks — or any other interlocking children's toy — can be used as a graphic portrayal of software data transmission, says Maureen Bundy, senior network instructor for GTE.

Most software is written to be loaded into memory in layers, and to interlock with layers above and below. She says Legos are excellent object lessons, especially since software functions are often difficult to learn because they're not visual.

For a team exercise, Legos can be labeled with appropriate computer commands or functions, separated into bags, and given to teams to reconstruct in the proper sequence.

Sometimes the most creative way to present material is merely to kill an old habit, says consultant Ray Roberts of Dayton, OH.

In product training, the presenter usually talks about the product's components, reveals the benefits it provides, and — if the gizmo is smaller than a breadbox — passes it through the audience.

Roberts says this is a good method if you're training just one person, but suggests that this hard-to-resist method should be avoided with larger groups because it creates audience commotion. "One-half of the group won't understand how it works, one-fourth won't care how it works, and the other one-fourth will be telling each other how they *think* it works."

Roberts recommends showing the product features on an overhead screen. Explain what they are, how they work, and what they do for the user.

"If it's important that the trainees touch, feel, taste, or smell it, let them know the product will be available for examination *after* the presentation."

10

Making products available after class avoids commotion

11

Disturbance list prevents classroom 'sabotage'

Tom Coroeneveld, training coordinator for the Ontario Ministry of Labor, takes his participants through a "sabotage" exercise. He has them list all the ways to disturb or make the workshop unbearable for him and other attendees. The list is posted, and when any of these behaviors occur, individual class members can point out that the behavior is disturbing or "sabotaging" the class.

Lecture is not the only way — or necessarily the best way — to communicate to a class, says Janice Combest, adult education director for the Michigan Capitol Girl Scout Council.

She gives participants a group of questions to answer. They are allowed to use any resource in the room to find information — books, filmstrips, or other trainees.

After the activity, Combest asks, "How many people used *people* as a resource in finding answers to the questions?" She also asks how many used only their own knowledge and what they found through books and other reference materials.

Combest says the exercise helps those who often are too reliant on the trainer become more aware of the broader spectrum of resources available for meeting their needs and solving their problems.

12

Multiple resources offer options for overly reliant learners

13

Dividing room into 'learning levels' addresses varied needs

Trainer Toni La Motta of Tarrytown, NY, does participants a big favor by delineating the difficulty of the material she is presenting. She uses the "walk across the room" approach with groups that clearly have varying abilities, such as management classes that include managers-to-be *and* managers.

She tells participants that the right side of the room is where she will speak "techie" (or more advanced than needed) and the left side is where she will be more elementary. When she is in the middle of the room, everyone should be as attentive as possible, but each group gets a mental break when she goes to the opposite side. (Students tune out occasionally anyway, says La Motta, so why not help direct when?)

La Motta says newer students usually listen and stretch to understand when she tells them the learning is above them, and more advanced students may listen to review more elementary materials. She says she's never had participants say they were lost or bored as a result of the technique.

14

Preclass assignments pack in more learning

Preclass assignments can be an important element of a training program for which class time is limited. That's true for a one-day workshop aimed at helping employees determine if supervision is the right career choice for them, conducted by Sandra McKinney of the Higher Education Services Corp. of New York State.

Before the workshop, trainees are asked to read a supervisory text and conduct three interviews with managers about what new supervisors may face on the job.

The benefits:

• Starts trainees thinking about the subject before the workshop.

• Actively involves trainees in researching the topic.

• Cuts briefing and introductory class time.

• Gives trainees a common knowledge and experience base.

• Treats the trainees as adults responsible for their own learning.

• Tells "vacationers" that this is a *workshop*.

15

Inject humor into selecting group leaders

Here's a way for participants to creatively select small-group leaders:

Michael Hagen, area training and employment manager of Hallmark Cards, uses the "Point Plus" system. He asks team members to quickly point to the person they want as leader. The person with the most fingers pointing at her assumes she'll be speaking or taking the leadership responsibility for the group throughout the seminar.

But Hagen then adds a twist by informing the group that the Point Plus method means the "elected" leader has the privilege of turning to her left or right to select her new leader of choice.

16

'Role cards' teach trainers to handle difficult situations

President of White River Training Co., B.J. Bischoff, helps participants in a train-the-trainer course practice managing difficult attendees by asking each to lead a brief discussion. Before the discussion, the rest of the group selects "role" cards, some of which tell attendees to create as much disturbance as possible, and others which simply tell participants to act naturally.

Once the discussion is over, Bischoff analyzes the participant's ability to manage the difficult behavior, and also identifies the various behaviors observed. Participants then reveal their role cards and discuss how they exhibited the behaviors. The process is repeated until every participant has been a discussion leader.

17

'Tag team' approach to role-plays keeps participants attentive

A different twist on role-plays is guaranteed to keep participants attentive, says Shirley Poertner, staff consultant for training and development for Meredith Corp. Rather than using traditional role-plays for senior-level managers, Poertner uses a "tag-team" approach.

She divides the managers into two groups of five participants each. Group A members are all given the script for one role, and Group B members are given the other half of the same role-play. One manager from each group begins the role-play, with the other four managers from each group lined up behind the one who is seated and playing the role.

At any point, the manager from either team in the role-play can reach behind and touch or "tag" any of the other managers standing behind them. At that point, the tagged team member steps forward and continues the role-play.

Poertner says the exercise is effective because all participants need to stay attentive so they're prepared to jump in.

A variation is for the waiting team members to take the initiative in tagging their way into the role-play.

18

Team-oriented role-plays create a supportive environment

Louis Rofrano, sales training manager at Baxter Healthcare, teaches salespeople perseverance with use of this role-play:

Each participant is given a towel. During a role-play of a sales situation, if the designated salesperson fails to adequately probe or loses control of the presentation, other group members can come to the rescue and "throw in their towels." Conversely, if the salesperson conducting the role-play feels it's futile to continue the sales pitch, he or she can quit by literally throwing in the towel.

Rofrano says the exercise keeps the group focused on the presentation, and encourages participants to be supportive of one another — something often lacking in a sales environment. "The last thing any salesperson wants to do," he says, "is throw in the towel — on himself or on an associate."

19

Telephone log captures anecdotes, ideas

Bill Weeks, a personnel analyst with the City of Los Angeles, keeps a telephone log specifically for recording interesting or amusing anecdotes he hears over the phone that he could incorporate in his presentations. The log reminds him to document material and has helped him compile current anecdotes for his classes.

Subtle approach gently rouses drowsy trainees

Robert Jolles, senior training specialist for Xerox International, is sympathetic to drowsy participants who seem on the verge of falling asleep during his presentations. It's a feeling he's experienced himself, so he has found a way to help his participants avoid the embarrassment of nodding off.

"Often students are doing everything in their power to stay awake, and given a choice, they would love not to humiliate themselves in front of the instructor and the rest of the class," Jolles says.

The old standard method, Jolles, says, is to move the presentation toward the person's desk and gradually raise your voice without calling attention to the napper. But for true snoozers, this subtle nudge won't last long. So Jolles keeps a pitcher of ice water and a few paper cups at hand. When a student begins to drift off, he pours a cup of water, moves around the room, and drops it off as he passes by the person's desk. He doesn't call any attention to the incident and continues to move along. "It sure beats throwing an eraser, and will be genially appreciated by your snoozer," he says.

21

Props help trainees focus on process

Cheri Stein, a training consultant in South Haven, MI, uses Tinkertoys in a seven-step demonstration process that she says results in smooth and logical explanations of new tasks and procedures. Using Tinkertoys, Stein says, instead of "real" products, allows trainees to attend more to the process than to the content.

Partners take turns being the trainer and trainee as they construct Tinkertoy products with the names Rootin' Tootin' Thingamabob, World Class Widget, Ever Popular Whatchamacallit, and World Famous Thingamajig. Stein gives the "trainer" a sheet of assembly instructions and gives both parties seven steps to follow:

1. *Trainer talks* — tells what will be covered, how the product works, why it is important, and so on.

2. *Trainer questions* — trainer asks questions of trainee to monitor learning, and answers any questions. This step continues throughout the session.

3. *Trainer demonstrates* — shows how to do a task three different times: Once at regular speed, once at slow speed, and once again at regular speed.

4. *Trainee talks* — summarizes what was covered, how the product

works, why it is important, etc.

5. *Trainee demonstrates* — with continual guidance and feedback from the trainer.

6. *Trainee demonstrates* — without guidance, and feedback only at the end of the task.

7. *Trainer follows-up* — checks back with trainee to smooth rough edges or answer questions.

22

Challenge trainees to implement a learning point right away

At the outset of her classes, trainer Jeryl Moy of CNA Insurance asks participants to consider during the class what they will immediately put into practice back on the job. She tells them to write down one or two of the most useful things they learn. At the end of the session, she asks each person to share what they have written. Moy cites these benefits:

• The exercise acts as a review of almost every important point covered during the session.

• It allows participants to put in their own words what they learned and how they will use it. This clarifies the points for them and enhances the likelihood they will apply them.

When Steve Trouba, regional training consultant for McDonald's, Kansas City, MO, tells participants to pick a number from one to 10 to determine their next group leader, he doesn't really have a number in mind. He says it is important for him to take the initiative — if someone hasn't yet been the leader, or if he thinks a certain person will lead the group to the conclusion he expects — Trouba simply tells that person he or she guessed the number.

23

Involve everyone when choosing group leaders

24

Goal-setting cements commitment to apply learning

Bonnie Higbee, quality improvement trainer for Boeing Aerospace & Electronics, suggests ending goal-setting sessions by having trainees immediately apply their newly acquired goal-setting knowledge.

Higbee divides the class into triads. He has them set short-term career goals, which they share with their groups. The members of the triads give feedback on the clarity of the goals and offer additional tips to expand the goals or to find resources to help them reach their goals.

25

Engaging introduction sets stage for course content

An introductory exercise for a train-the-trainer session for managers at United National Bank & Trust Co., Canton, OH, sets the stage for an explanation of the course content and its importance. Barbara Heinricher, training and customer relations officer at United National Bank, splits the class into three groups — trainers, trainees, and customers. Each group receives an index card with a specific situation and question written on it, designed to help identify its needs.

Trainer Group: You have "volunteered" to train your staff on a new product or procedure. What do you need to know in order to fulfill your assignment?

Trainee Group: You are a staff member and have been told you will be trained on new product information. How do you want to learn the material?

Customer Group: You are a customer. What do you expect the staff to know about the new product the organization is advertising?

She records responses on a flip chart or transparency and then shares the results with the entire group. By changing the situations and questions, she uses the same format to introduce a variety of training topics.

26

Encourage trainees to 'hang in there' to see skill improvement

Susan Boyd, director of corporate support and development at PC Concepts, Wayne, PA, uses this exercise to show participants how unfamiliarity with a task or job can affect performance:

Ask participants to write a word related to the course topic. Time one person to see how long the task takes.

Then ask participants to switch to their other hand and write the word again. Time the same person to get a comparative example. Boyd observes the following reactions by trainees: expressions like, "You've got to be kidding!" nervous laughter, hesitance to start, reluctance to try, writing with their other hand then switching back to their writing hand, higher concentration levels, and carefully watching the pen and the word being formed.

Talk about the results. Typically writing the word takes about four to six seconds the first time, and about twice as long with the other hand. Ask the class why it took so long the second time. Then ask participants to analyze the quality of the second writing sample. Obviously, it looks worse than the first sample.

Boyd closes by relating the exercise to learning. She tells the class that if they lost the use of their writing hand, what they just experienced would happen over the first two or three weeks as they started to learn how to write with their other hand. By the fourth week, they would see improvement in the time and quality of their writing. By the end of four to six months, they would no longer see a difference, as they would have assimilated the new skill and become adept and comfortable using their other hand.

In conclusion, Boyd relates the exercise to a new topic or skill taught in the class. She tells attendees that the next two or three weeks will be the hardest, because doing tasks with a new technique will seem to take more time, require more effort, and still may not meet their quality standards.

She encourages them to hang in there, because once they get past the three-week hurdle, they will see a tremendous improvement in both time and quality as the new learning is assimilated into their daily routines.

27

Telling real-life stories succinctly introduces learning points

A point some trainers may overlook when struggling to involve trainees in their sessions is that trainees can often convey a learning point better than the instructor can. The lesson? It's not only important to get individuals involved for their *own* sake, but for the sake of the group and the learning objectives.

• Herb Burton, advisory instructor for IBM in Ontario, Canada, often asks for a volunteer (or he chooses someone) to relate an experience about a point he intends to make. When the "volunteer" tells the story, the student makes Burton's point before he presents it, so when he addresses the issue it is reinforcement rather than an introduction of a point. This emphasizes the lesson, and creates audience participation and empathy.

• Tommy Coolesey, training instructor for Wackenhut Services Inc. of Aiken, SC, recommends researching the job backgrounds of some participants before a course begins. Then, when you want to make a particular point, you have a good idea of which participants might have relevant experiences. Coolesey says this tactic also encourages networking among class members.

In her customer service classes, Kathy Schoenberg, training specialist in Brooklyn Center, MN, puts trainees in the customers' place.

Many customers can be overwhelmed by terms they are not familiar or comfortable with, and may not be bold enough to ask for clarification for fear of appearing ignorant. With that in mind, Schoenberg sets up a "Customer Service Titivation" session.

On the first day, she asks participants if they know the meaning of titivation (to make smart or spruce up). One or two people in each session did not know but look up the meaning, and the others plead ignorance or think it is a typographical error (motivation).

That opener leads to a discussion of how the terms and procedures they use every day are not necessarily common knowledge to customers. Schoenberg also points out the small ratio of participants who looked the word up, comparing that to the many customers who are also hesitant to research something or ask questions when they're confused. This exercise encourages employees to ask customers if they want an explanation of cloudy terms or procedures.

28

Remind participants to explain cloudy terms

29

Tapping devilish creativity gets trainees' attention

This inventive opener from Dick Schultz, lead instructor for the security operations committee of Wackenhut Services, Aiken, SC, is not easily applied to all audiences or classrooms. But his point is that trainers sometimes need to let go of their inhibitions and rely on the devilish creativity that falls outside the realm of normal ice breakers and attention-getters.

Schultz opens a class for security personnel who need to master the quick repair of broken windows by walking into the classroom — which has one wall made up entirely of small window panes — carrying a golf club, a strip of artificial turf, and a golf ball. Without a word, Schultz lays out the turf, places the ball on it, and calmly hits the ball through a pane of glass.

He then moves to a table where he has preset his presentation tools — window panes, glass, putty, and putty knives — and class begins.

Rather than coaching speakers to "speak from their diaphragms," Janice Pierce, area manager for education with Southwestern Bell in Irving, TX, simply advises them to stand up straight and hold in their stomachs. The strategy makes people automatically use their stomach muscles rather than their throat muscles when speaking. Pierce says this method also helps most people maintain good, strong volume.

30

Use your stomach for greater volume

31

Show trainees the pitfalls of 'selective listening'

James Shadel, instructor with GPU Nuclear of Middletown, PA, uses this opening exercise to demonstrate how preconceived ideas prevent us from hearing what others want to communicate:

Shadel prints the letters:

WSODTROW

on the board or a flip chart. He then gives everyone a piece of paper and tells them to form two words from the letters. After allowing a few minutes to write, he has participants share their results.

Very few people will use the letters to write: "TWO WORDS," as instructed. Most, he says, don't dare challenge preconceived notions that filter our communications. Schadel makes the point that every message passes through a series of filters — sender, message, receiver — which vary depending on sex, age, trade, or other characteristics of the communicators involved. Awareness of the filters, Shadel says, can greatly improve communication.

To help reinforce product-knowledge training back on the job, Theresa Dunlap, trainer at United National Bank, Vienna, WV, hides clues in the company's weekly employee newsletter. Dunlap places four or five simple one- or two-word clues throughout the newsletter — in unrelated articles or hidden in line art graphics — that point to one specific product or service trainees have learned in the past.

Then, posing as the "Super Sleuth Phantom Caller," Dunlap selects a few people each week and calls them to see if they can identify the "Mystery Product of the Week." All of the calls, she says, are made with the theme music of *The Pink Panther* playing in the background.

Not only does this technique reinforce product knowledge, Dunlap says, it also stresses the importance of reading the newsletter weekly. Winners are awarded a cash prize, and their names are posted in the newsletter.

32

Ingenious techniques reinforce product knowledge

33

Mock interviews help develop fact-finding skills

In sales or other training courses that involve honing fact-finding skills, this exercise used by Victoria Hart, training manager for TeleDirect Publications of Scarborough, Ontario, may serve as a catalyst for discussion.

Hart writes the names of celebrities on index cards. She has each trainee pick a card and consider how they would interview that celebrity. Ask participants to first come up with one easy-to-answer question they would use to break the ice. Then have participants produce two questions of a more critical or penetrating nature. Next have each participant share his or her questions and reasons why they would ask them.

The exercise, Hart says, helps illustrate the importance of easing into the "fact finding" stage of a sales call and of asking thought-provoking questions that involve the customer.

34

Before- and after-training videos make a point about preparation

Lori Addicks, program development manager at Glasrock Home Health Care, Atlanta, GA, make a point about the importance of preparation and familiarity with subject matter in making quality presentations with this exercise:

She has each participant list six things that capture the essence of their personalities — hobbies or interests — on a sign titled "I Am." Participants then silently circulate through the room wearing their signs, and reading other participants' signs as they circulate.

Participants then pair off and prepare to introduce each other to the group with further information gleaned through conversation about the "I Am" lists. Addicks videotapes the introductions, then replays them while mentioning the difficulty of presenting an unfamiliar topic.

At the conclusion of the course, participants are videotaped again making presentations about themselves based on one or more of their "I Am" items. Addicks then has participants compare their own presentations.

35

Experiencing teamwork helps participants understand roles

This "Get through the Window" exercise can enhance team-building, says Dee Endelman, manager of human resources at Puget Sound Air Pollution Control in Seattle:

1. Break the group into a few teams and tell the teams to take a break together.

2. Cut two pieces of flip-chart paper into the shape of "c's" and tape them together to create a "window" (shown below).

3. Tape the window across the door frame of the room, high enough so participants will need help getting through, and post a sign stating, "Get your team through the window without breaking it."

Get through the Window Exercise

Training 101
Get your team through the window without breaking it.

4. Call a team back. Observe discreetly as they work to solve the problem.

5. When the team is through the window, conduct a discussion on who did what in the process and how the others reacted to one another's roles.

Endelman says she often uses the exercise at department/management retreats because it provides people within work groups an avenue of communication in a nonthreatening environment.

36

Don't let trainees coast through training

Ongoing certification programs or regular refresher courses can lull participants into a false sense of security, says Zelma Newlin, course development specialist at Abbott Laboratories, Irving, TX. While they might *think* they know it all, the mind has a tendency not to pay attention to things that have become commonplace. To illustrate that danger and to encourage constant attention to detail, Newlin uses the following exercise:

She puts the group into pairs and asks one person to take off his watch and give it to his partner. Then, while it is concealed by his partner, the first person attempts to provide a written description of the watch. The watch owner then reads the description aloud and her partner checks the accuracy of the description, which Newlin says is often far enough off-base to make participants realize how little attention they pay to something they might look at dozens of times a day.

37

Modeling improper behaviors illustrates need for coping skills

As an introduction to a front-line leadership session called "Dealing with the Emotional Employee," Jim Perkins, a human resource manager with Prince Corp., Holland, MI, uses this technique to make a point:

Just before the end of an ice breaker mixer, Perkins contradicts something he previously announced to the group about not allowing unnecessary interruptions during a training session. He excuses himself to answer an internal page. When he returns, he comes in abruptly and noticeably disturbed, dropping books as he enters. Then he takes off on an emotional outburst about some fabricated happening for one to three minutes.

He stops just as abruptly as he started, sits down, and asks participants, "How do you feel right now, and why?" He says the exercise leads the class into a frank discussion about dealing with emotional employees and their outbursts, removes inhibitions, and encourages people to relax and take risks.

38

Groups work best when all participate equally

To build group decision-making skills and teach group dynamics, Lucia Shillito, with the Australian Taxation Department, splits her participants into groups of five or six. After choosing a series of discussion topics related to the course, she gives each group a large piece of butcher's paper and one marker.

The person who speaks first holds the marker, draws a connecting line on the paper to the next person who speaks, then hands the marker to

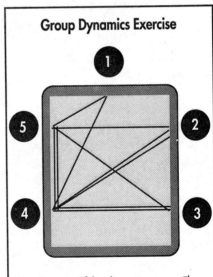

Group Dynamics Exercise

The dynamics of this discussion group: The lines indicate that Participant #4 dominated the conversation, while Participant #1 was involved very little.

that person. Each time someone contributes, the marker is passed and another connecting line is drawn, producing a maze of lines as the group completes the discussion. After a debriefing of the discussion, the group examines the story told by the pattern of lines — who dominated discussion, who didn't participate as frequently, and why.

In a discussion of group dynamics, Shillito emphasizes the need for people to draw each other into participating, so there is balance in discussions and no one member dominates.

39

Presenting role-plays before one-person audience decreases anxieties

To lower participants' anxieties about role-playing and skill practice, Donna Franz, director of training and development with Ameritech Publishing in Troy, MI, breaks the class into two groups — deliverers and receivers — and pairs them up. The receivers sit in a circle, chairs facing out. Each deliverer stands, faces a receiver, and speaks only to that person.

After about two minutes Franz stops the activity and asks each receiver to write down one idea that will help the deliverer improve. Deliverers rotate to the right and repeat the process, incorporating receivers' suggestions. This continues until each deliverer has demonstrated for each receiver. Roles are reversed and the process repeated.

The exercise allows participants to practice a skill before a critical audience without having to face the "stage fright" that performing before the full class might present.

40

Exploring 'initial' needs clarifies trainee expectations

Susan Hauser, an education specialist at Deluxe Data Systems Inc., Brown Deer, WI, uses this exercise to familiarize participants with one another and to give her information about their course expectations:

She asks students to use each of their initials to answer a question. For example she might ask them to describe one thing they'd like to learn from the program using their first initials (S — Several new training techniques). Using their middle initials, she asks them to describe their greatest challenge relating to the course topic (F — Focus; maintaining student focus). Using their last initials, participants are asked to share one interesting fact about themselves (H — Honesty; I like people to tell me the truth).

41

Defining roles early clears way for learning

To address possible resistance from attendees and to clearly define the roles of the participant and instructor, Jim Lee, a sales training manager for Warner Lambert, Morris Plains, NJ, begins his classes with this explanation:

"Let's talk about roles — yours and mine. First, yours: You can view your part as being on vacation, where you will just sit back and relax, or that you are here as a prisoner — where your boss says you must be. I hope you are here to learn.

"Now, mine: You can think of me as a teacher, which I am not. You can view me as an expert, but I am not that either. Rather, I am a guide to lead you through the material. If I cannot personally answer a question, I will find out and get back to you."

Lee says the clarification helps put the trainer at ease for not being perfect, and also allows the participants to relax and know the instructor is human, too.

42

Juggling scarves illustrates interaction of concepts

Juggling scarves can be mastered in as little as 10 minutes, says Linda Sacha, owner of Discovery Seminars in Palm City, FL, and produces a much more dramatic effect than juggling tennis balls or bean bags.

"It's a fabulous closing to summarize each of three main points with scarves and then illustrate the importance of all three concepts interacting with the final juggle.

To juggle, hold two objects in your right hand and one in your left. Throw one from your right hand in an arc so that it will land in your left. While the first object is airborne, throw the one in your left hand in an arc across to your right hand. After you have caught the first object and before you catch the second, throw the third object in an arc from right to left. To continue, alternate throws from one hand to the other. Higher arcs are easier until you get the hang of juggling.

43

Group exercises fill learning gaps individuals overlook

When detailed or complex procedures are part of a process, the collective thinking of a group can fill in learning gaps individuals may miss, says Sandi Spivey, field training manager for KFC National Management Co. in Santa Ana, CA.

When participants bring some experience to a training session and must learn or refine a procedure that requires a sequence of steps, Spivey suggests this exercise:

She gives stacks of 3 x 5 inch index cards (Post-it Notes may also be used) to participants and asks them to write the sequence of tasks needed to complete a project (for example, a list of tasks needed to open a restaurant as a manager).

When each has completed three to six cards, writing one task per card, she collects the cards, sticks them to the wall, and reads them to the group. Spivey then asks the group to look for "holes" in the sequence of duties and writes down each new idea on a card and adds it to the other ideas. She assigns two or three people to sort cards by their specific sequence. She adds "headers" (in this case: by 7 a.m., by 8 a.m., etc.) and tasks normally completed in that time are placed under the appropriate headings.

The exercise, Spivey says, allows the group to clarify and refine a sequence and learn from each other. At the close of the activity, the cards may be removed from the walls, and distributed among the group so participants can summarize and copy the steps.

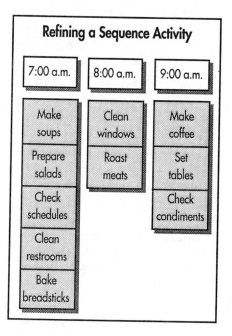

Refining a Sequence Activity

7:00 a.m.	8:00 a.m.	9:00 a.m.
Make soups	Clean windows	Make coffee
Prepare salads	Roast meats	Set tables
Check schedules		Check condiments
Clean restrooms		
Bake breadsticks		

44

Wearing personnel managers' shoes gives trainees new perspective

This management development exercise is used to help trainees make difficult personnel decisions. Barbara Graham, dean of the Baton Rouge School of Computers, Baton Rouge, LA, uses it as an activity opener or as a method to inspire and involve trainees.

She calls the activity "Who Stays?" Trainees are asked to pretend they are top management and must soon lay off employees due to market conditions. She gives each trainee an identical list of 15 imaginary employees, with detailed job descriptions and other variables, such as personalities and accomplishments. She tells trainees the company can only keep 10 of the 15 and they must decide who stays. If the group is large, Graham assigns groups of three to work together.

After each group makes their decisions, descriptions of each employee are read aloud and a count is recorded of how many chose to keep each person. After a group-wide decision is made on the layoffs, the group explores why they made those decisions.

Graham says the exercise "brings out the many admired traits of good employees and also makes the group aware of characteristics not tolerated by most companies."

At the beginning of his classes, Salvatore Spataro, a trainer with the Visionary Group, Nepean, Ontario, tells participants goal setting is difficult, but that it can be the most powerful tool for reaching goals. To help trainees focus on the keys of successful goal setting, Spataro first teaches his classes their goals must be "S.M.A.R.T.":

Specific — Will I know when I reach my goal?

Measurable — Can I tell if I'm moving toward my goal?

Attainable — What is the probability that I can reach this goal?

Realistic — Has anyone every done this or is it doable?

Truth — Do I really want to do this?

Next, he discusses determining what obstacles exist and how to deal with them. He encourages participants to ask themselves, "Why have I not reached that goal so far? What must I overcome?" Once the obstacles are identified, Spataro has participants log the action steps they must complete to reach their goals.

45

Help trainees focus on successful goal-setting keys

46

Encourage trainees to learn first hand from line workers

A contest modeled after a road rally teaches employees at all levels about the company's manufacturing process in an enjoyable way, says Kerrie Blanch, employee development manager at Sterling Pharmaceuticals, Ermington, Australia.

First she pairs up attendees, preferably with people from different divisions or organizational levels, to facilitate broad networking. She tells the group the material she is about to present will be important in completing the exercise that will follow. Blanch then presents 20 minutes of information on the manufacturing division's structure, and on "good manufacturing processes."

Next she gives each pair of participants a copy of a questionnaire. Some answers will have been provided by her lecture. Others must be gleaned from workers on the factory floor.

The partners follow the question sheet as it guides them to different areas of the factory. They are encouraged to ask equipment operators for help. The team that completes the form first wins the race.

Proper posture facilitates learning

Students who sit or stand for an extended period of time generally do not use correct posture and, as a result, do not learn at an optimal level, says Richard Way, coaching coordinator for the British Columbia Sporting and Recreation Division, Victoria, British Columbia. To enhance posture he periodically "resets" his participants' bodies.

After an activity that requires movement he instructs participants to put their backs firmly against the back of their chairs, chest out, shoulders back, head square on top of their shoulders, and knees together. This, he says, enhances hormonal release in the body, which facilitates learning.

48

Have trainees provide a barometer of class needs

Judy Johnson, a trainer for the State of Alabama Department of Human Resources, Montgomery, AL, gets a feel for the needs of participants in her supervisory training program and helps them get to know one another by having them issue "weather forecasts" for their departments.

She first asks participants to identify on paper what season of the year they are in as supervisors. A spring supervisor is one who has just been planted. A summer supervisor is fairly new, but growing. An autumn supervisor is well-established and learning to weather storms. A winter supervisor is experienced and interested in fertilizing new growth.

Next she has them use weather terminology to describe the atmosphere of their departments. If all is smooth, warm and sunny might be the forecast. If the department is in a period of change, the forecast might call for windy weather.

Johnson asks participants to read their answers to the class. She records them on a flip chart. This method lets people know where they stand in comparison to others, and lets the instructor tailor the delivery to match students' needs and experience levels, she says.

Groups don't necessarily need a traditional leader to function effectively. Lucia Shillito, a trainer in the Australian Taxation Department stresses that point in her leadership and team-building training sessions.

When working with groups of at least 15 or 20 trainees, Shillito asks the whole group to "huddle" together in one corner of the room. She has them stand so they can place a hand on the shoulder of another trainee. Together, she says, they represent one life form — an amoeba, for example. The only way the "amoeba" can move is by each trainee releasing one person's shoulder and touching someone else's shoulder. Each person must keep moving in this way. The group's goal is to arrive at the other end of the room through some sort of fabricated passageway — a gauntlet formed by lined-up chairs, for instance, that is smaller than the width of the group.

Shillito says no one person can "lead" the group — it must lead itself via coordinated teamwork.

49

Show trainees no single person can 'lead' a team

50

Class 'experts' maximize shared learning

This exercise helps large groups of trainees develop and then share specific areas of expertise among themselves. Ron Gabinet, a trainer in Alberta, Canada, has participants number off at their tables (one through five) to match the five content areas to be discussed. Each number is assigned a topic and those with similar numbers sit together for discussion. After 20 to 30 minutes, participants break up their topic groups and reconvene at their original tables. The "expert" for each topic leads a discussion sharing information on that topic. Gabinet says the sharing typically includes things like a chapter or segment of a pertinent resource manual.

To enliven the usually mundane task of asking participants what questions they have coming into a training session, Vickie Iverson, an instructor at CPI, Arden Hills, MN, developed a "Dear Trainer" exercise. Based on the popular "Dear Abby" advice column in newspapers, Iverson does the following:

About a week before the class, she surveys attendees to determine questions they have that specifically relate to the course material.

With this information in hand, she prepares a list of questions representative of those she has received, as well as answers or suggestions relevant to the questions.

Iverson then writes each question on an individual piece of paper, starting each with "Dear Trainer,..." and signs them with creative monikers such as "Perplexed in Payroll."

She puts all the question sheets into a box decorated as the classroom mailbox. Throughout the course, Iverson asks participants to draw "letters" from the mailbox and read them to the class. She then forms small groups to brainstorm action ideas to solve the problem or answer the question. She collects their ideas and presents her own at the end of the allotted time.

51

Creative questions elicit better trainee responses

52

Add spice to learning acronyms

One element of many types of training — orientation, technical, and new product, for example — includes teaching attendees the full meaning of acronyms used by a company. Deb Hartford, training coordinator for the Harris Corp., Lincoln, NE, adds a little spice to the exercise of presenting acronyms and their definitions by using a game she calls "Best Guess."

Hartford pairs attendees, presents each team with a list of acronyms (however many are appropriate to the training), and asks them to come up with their best guesses as to what the acronyms stand for, using any prior knowledge or just plain common sense. After five minutes, she asks the teams to set their lists aside and proceed with the session.

At the end of the course, she asks teams to review their best guesses and determine how many acronyms they correctly identified. Hartford presents a can of alphabet soup to the team with the most correct answers, telling them they earned all 26 letters for being so astute. To the second place team, Hartford awards each with an individual serving package of Cheerios, telling them they only get the letter O.

If you're uncomfortable saying, "I'll have to get back to you on that one," when you are unable to answer a question, try this solution, suggested by Linda Brawley, a sales and management development specialist for Great Western Bank, San Diego.

At the beginning of class, tack a piece of flip-chart paper to the wall with the title, "Stump the Trainer," and challenge participants to come up with questions you won't be able to answer. When a participant comes up with a stumper, have the trainee write it on the flip chart and then promise the class you'll get the answer by a specific time.

To get the answer on time, schedule a break and check with a subject expert or reference materials. This method saves your credibility, demonstrates the importance of not guessing at answers, and shows you can keep a promise. It also helps engage students in the material as they search for challenging questions.

53

Challenge trainees to 'stump the trainer'

54

Sketches help trainees express feelings about change

When a company is undergoing a lot of internal change — be it a downsizing or a new management philosophy — Mary Maloney, a sales training development manager at DataServ in Eden Prairie, MN, feels it's important for employees to get their emotions and thoughts on the table.

To solicit those feelings from salespeople, she uses the following exercise. In groups of two to four, she has each trainee draw an automobile that depicts or describes the current state of the company. They discuss the drawings in the small groups. Then Maloney asks for volunteers to describe their drawings to the class and explain why they chose certain features. For example, some have drawn sports cars with oversized steering wheels — depicting a fast-moving organization with traditional command and control management — to autos with large rearview mirrors to depict leaving the bad times behind.

Len Whiting, manager of business education at Whirlpool Corp., Benton Harbor, MI, uses buddy sheets to ensure that participants use training back on the job to achieve predetermined goals and to foster networking.

During training Whiting encourages trainees to meet at least one new person in class. He then has these partners exchange action plans or lists of things they plan to do for the next 90 days, one year, and three years. The buddies are urged to follow-up on each other at 30-day intervals to see how well they are reaching the goals on their buddy sheets.

55

'Buddy system' promotes follow-up, networking

56

Standards-based performance evaluations prove less stressful

Evaluating employees' performance is a stressful but necessary part of a manager's job. David Valade, a training center instructor for Taco Bell Corp., Chicago, says this technique helps management trainees understand the process better, thereby easing the strain:

Each participant gets a sheet of paper, tears it in half and prints the word "standard" on the top of one piece. Next, each neatly signs the labeled piece. Finally, each participant "duplicates" the first signature on the remaining blank sheet.

Valade asks attendees to compare the signatures side-by-side. Participants generally find the two identical or nearly so. He then asks them to compare the signatures by placing the second sheet on top of the "standard" sheet and trying to align signatures by holding the papers up to the light. Participants find that perfect alignment is impossible.

The lesson: Managers need a thorough understanding of their company's employee standards, and should compare employees not against one another, but against those standards. This is easier and less stressful than comparing people against one another.

To teach participants the value of recognizing and addressing the sensitive issue of group dynamics in the workplace, Samantha Doly, staff training officer for the AMP Society, Brisbane, Australia, breaks the class into groups of four or five and assigns each a problem that must be solved by consensus. She tells the groups that while they work on the problem, she will place customized baseball caps on the heads of three attendees in each group. The hats are labeled:

- Know It All — Ignore Me
- Expert — Listen to Me
- Insecure — Encourage Me

Doly instructs group members to treat the people wearing the hats according to the labels, although each person wearing a cap is unaware of what the cap says.

When forced to deal with those dynamics, Doly says, groups rarely reach consensus within the 10-minute time limit she sets. The point of the exercise, she says, is to teach participants to constantly be on the lookout for differing personalities that might affect a group.

57

Sensitize trainees to impact of various personalities on group

58

Firsthand experiences increase sensitivity to diversity

To foster awareness of and sensitivity to diversity, Roseanne Brenna, director of training at Howard Johnson Hotels and Lodges, Wayne, NJ, divides classes into four groups. Each group is given an activity designed to simulate a particular performance barrier.

Group 1 takes notes from an audio cassette on instructions being given by a trainer — who happens to be bilingual. Only 75 percent of what the instructor says is in English; key action words are given in Spanish or any other language foreign to most participants. The activity, Brenna says, helps participants realize the frustration of not understanding English in an English-dominant environment.

Group 2 threads needles and sews buttons on scraps of fabric with their dominant eyes closed to demonstrate vision impairment. (To determine which eye is dominant, ask participants to make a circle with a thumb and forefinger, hold it at arm's length, focus on an object through the circle, then close one eye. If the object and circle are still aligned, the open eye is the dominant one.) This activity simulates everyday problems faced by people with sight problems.

Group 3 listens to a tape at varying volumes while wearing ear plugs. This activity illustrates the challenges presented by hearing impairment.

Group 4 members wrap, tape, and address their class binders for mailing — while wearing gardening gloves. The exercise recreates some of the difficulties of functioning with hands impaired by arthritis or other afflictions.

Each group watches as the others perform their tasks. Afterward, Brenna leads a discussion of participants' feelings during the exercise, including the frustration and first-time awareness of the difficulties of "walking in another's shoes."

Section Two: Learner Motivation Techniques

Sherry Boyd, human resource manager for Fireman's Fund Insurance, creates positive networking and encourages people to learn from each other through a quiz exercise with a twist.

At the beginning of a course she distributes a 20-question quiz, and offers a prize for the first attendee who finishes with no errors. She then announces that before the course she gave five participants the answers to five different questions. The twist: Those participants are allowed to cheat and give answers to classmates only if they're asked during breaks.

59

Letting attendees 'cheat' fosters networking

60

Compiling, distributing ideas trainees enact change

Immediately after a workshop, Elizabeth Schiff, senior training manager for the American Academy of Ophthalmology, collects all ideas recorded on flip-chart pages, compiles them into cohesive categories, and then distributes them to all participants a few weeks after the course.

She even goes to the extent of photocopying the ideas on hole-punched paper so attendees can add them to their course handout binder. Schiff says the "Captured Comments" ensure that no good ideas are lost and remind participants to continue to focus on ideas from the session.

One simple fact of life is that due to the difference between our rate of speech (about 175 words per minute) and our rate of aural comprehension (about 310 words per minute), people tend to mentally check in and out when listening to a speaker. This is often referred to as "leapfrogging," and can frustrate a trainer whose material requires extensive questioning and facilitation.

Relax, says Robert Jolles, senior training specialist with Xerox International. Leapfrogging is natural and — to a limited extent — should be expected. The real danger is when a student is asked a question and has no idea how to answer.

With that in mind, Jolles devised the "Leap Chip." Every day each student is given a two-inch disk. Once a day, for any reason a student cannot respond when called upon — leapfrogging, daydreaming, or simply not knowing an answer — he or she must hand the instructor the leap chip. It's important the instructor not break stride and in no way call attention to the incident, Jolles says.

61

Gentle 'prod' keeps participants tuned in

62

Addressing smoldering feelings puts out fire in hostile groups

Dealing with resistant groups is not unusual for most trainers. But sometimes, as Charlotte Donaldson, education specialist for Newtrend, puts it: "The natives aren't restless, they're downright hostile."

Donaldson finds she can neutralize an uncomfortable situation by including these questions in her introduction:

• On a scale of 1 to 10, how well do you currently understand the product/topic of this training?

• On a scale of 1 to 10, how well do you understand the product's (or topic's) documentation?

• What has been most frustrating in learning this product/topic?

Donaldson says this procedure clears the air before the class even begins. Students are asked to look for some things they already know, and she doesn't have to agree with what they say; she simply acknowledges their right to have certain feelings. The exercise addresses those smoldering feelings and enables participants to then be more receptive to her curriculum, says Donaldson.

Nancy Jackson, director of membership for the Heart of Missouri Girl Scouts, believes trainers should be more generous with recognition given during courses. It is more meaningful, she says, to have an employee- or volunteer-of-the-month award than to thank somebody for years of contribution at the end of a tenure.

The same is true for training programs. It's much more effective to give frequent and numerous smaller rewards than to simply recognize people for their contributions at the end of a lengthy training program.

63

Immediate recognition motivates participants

64

Brainstorm as group to elicit most-complete solutions

Ron Koch, a Mt. Prospect, IL-based trainer, uses this method to involve participants so they will feel ownership of class material:

Whenever there is a conflict or a problem situation within the material that needs a resolution, he presents the case before the class and asks for suggested solutions. Koch believes that when the class is given an opportunity to brainstorm, they learn because they already "own" the answer.

If there is a moment of silence, he doesn't break it. That silence works to motivate the students to contribute to the discussion, he says. He then writes their answers on the board with very little editorial comment. After all solutions are on the board, he takes a moment to help participants realize that, as a class working together, they found a viable solution.

Koch says the most important steps for using this activity effectively are:

1. Allow silence while class members ponder possible solutions.

2. If you're wondering if the answer fits, ask the class.

3. When finished, summarize what happened — that a unified group often has more brainpower than people working individually.

S ometimes we are so busy teaching content that we don't pause to encourage people to reflect on what they are learning. Participants can benefit from short periods to simply sit and digest what they've learned and how they might apply it.

From time to time designate two or three minutes as "application thought time." Suggest that participants write down the learning points from a presentation just delivered, or write out their own action ideas.

Background music may facilitate the process and enhance reflection time. Pieces such as Vivaldi's *Four Seasons*, Halpern's *Spectrum Suite*, or Kitaro's *Silk Road* can provide an effective background for reflection.

65

'Digestion time' lets trainees contemplate how to apply learning

66

Creativity award reinforces numerous learning points

K eedoozle represents creativity in action during training conducted by Lynn Baker, training manager at Fleming Co. Inc.

Keedoozle roughly means tongue-in-cheek fun, says Baker. It's really a tiny gold star stuck on a certificate of completion, but this "stellar" award sets the stage for up to eight learning opportunities.

For example, in a management by objectives (MBO) workshop, after providing an overview the first day, Baker announces one team will win a special award — the Keedoozle Award — when the class covers the topic of "innovative objectives." No other details are offered.

The next day Baker reviews and demonstrates guidelines for innovative objectives. Then teams have 45 minutes to reach agreement on one "best" innovative objective (with accompanying action plans) and to prepare a presentation.

Next, each team makes its presentation. Then, using the recommended guidelines as criteria, class members vote for the best innovation. Members cannot vote for their own team's entry.

Members of the winning team each receive a gold star, labeled "Keedoozle Award Winner," on their certificates.

Baker says the activity is effective because:

1. The end-of-the-day announcement creates suspense and encourages reflection on the innovative process.

2. Class members witness repeated demonstrations and reinforcement of learning as teams make their presentations.

3. The process of innovation is rewarded in class as a practice encouraged in the workplace.

4. A touch of relevant history is brought into the classroom: Keedoozle was the name of a daring innovation in grocery supermarkets by a pioneer in the industry, Clarence Saunders, founder of the Piggly Wiggly grocery chain.

5. Managers gain insights into each others' real-world concerns and proposed solutions.

6. The class also learns: (a) effects of time constraints on teams (b) how competition for incentives affects participants (c) effect of team pooling of ideas versus individual efforts (d) the implications for managing the MBO process.

7. The class has some belly laughs. It's fun.

8. Real-world innovations are conceived and attempted as a result of this session.

67

Show trainees taking risks is crucial to learning

To reinforce the idea that we learn from our mistakes, Don Moritz, workshop instructor for Florist's Transworld Delivery Association (FTD), begins training sessions by having participants introduce themselves by sharing the most successful experience they've had in their jobs, and their greatest mistakes, setbacks, or failures. Each person then shares what they learned from the failure and what they would do differently in the future.

Following this introduction, Moritz then leads a discussion of risk-taking and failure as being a natural process and part of professional growth. The exercise also helps participants focus on self-assessment as an effective management tool and experience as a good teacher.

Friendly competition for a classroom version of "Academy Awards" can enliven a group that must do a lot of role-plays, says Robert Jolles, senior training specialist for Xerox International.

He lays the ground rules at the beginning of the session: Each day a participant will be voted as a winner of some sort based on certain criteria such as "most improved," "best overall," "best job of implementing a new tactic taught," and so on.

A traveling trophy, such as a Frisbee or placard hung on the winner's chair, is passed on to a new winner at the end of each day. Jolles recommends a lighthearted award — his classes sometimes use a mug that reads, "For today, I'm as good as Rob."

The daily winner is awarded by determining such things as when the class should take breaks, time allotted for reading assignments, and other simple class decisions.

Because the criteria for selection is left wide open, Jolles says, the award can be spread around to all participants. As class members become more familiar with each other, the students begin to cheer for and assist those who haven't won an "award" yet.

68

Rewarding participants at all levels keeps motivation strong

69

Informal brainstorm session limbers up trainees' minds

As an exercise to stress the concept that no idea is a bad idea, Anita Lomurno, director of clinical education for HNS, asks small groups in brainstorming sessions to imagine they're entrepreneurs opening a store or restaurant. She challenges them to generate as many ideas — crazy or sane — as they can for marketing the new store or restaurant, and for designing its environment, facility, menu, and ambiance. Lomurno says the new "owners" of an imaginary fish store, for example, decided to promote their grand opening by sending a roving truck through the streets while playing the theme from "Jaws" over a loudspeaker.

Later in the course, when case studies require small-group problem-solving, Lomurno reminds participants of the exercise and the good ideas that came out of the uninhibited brainstorming. She says attendees often feel more comfortable with tossing out ideas as solutions to a problem if they've been through the more relaxed, informal exercise first.

When helping new trainees overcome their initial fears about actively participating in a training session, trainer Todd Anderson of the C.P. Morgan Co. asks his audience to close their eyes during his introductory comments.

Having the audience do this helps him manage his adrenaline surge and retain composure, but more importantly, says Anderson, it gets the audience in an active listening/thinking mood.

Anderson says this method also works well when teaching public speaking or presentation seminars. After participants are settled, he asks them to close their eyes and think of a time when they were asked to speak in public, to make a speech or a toast, or to perform in a play. "What were your initial feelings when you got up to speak?" he asks. The questions help to lead the group into a discussion on fears and adrenaline and how to overcome them.

70

Put your audience in an active listening mood

71

Make constructive use of gripes

Mark Hurst, health promotion specialist for EDS, asks two questions of anyone who makes a negative statement during a presentation or discussion:

• "Can this be changed, and if so, how?"

• "If it can't be changed, how can the person improve his or her acceptance of the contention?"

Hurst says that by directing all negative comments to these two questions, a gripe session is avoided and participants learn a method for alleviating resistance.

The Mistake Quota is a concept that Chuck Braun, psychometric division coordinator for Idea Connection Systems Inc., describes at the start of his classes as an aid to creating an open, trusting atmosphere and a way to relax a group right from the start.

Braun believes learning occurs best in an environment where people aren't afraid to try new things or to make mistakes. To that end, he says he will give each student a quota of 30 mistakes for the training session, and if they use those up he will give them 30 more. Braun says he can almost hear the sighs of relief in the room as people relax and begin participating.

72

Encouraging mistakes helps trainees open up

73

Stress reserving judgment during brainstorm sessions

Whistleblowing is encouraged by Anne Beninghof, trainer specialist for Capitol Region Education Council, in brainstorming activities. After reminding the participants of brainstorming rules (shoot for quantity, not quality; anything goes; hitchhiking on another idea is allowed; judgment of any kind is verboten), she puts the focus on the importance of reserving judgment.

To help keep this in mind throughout the activity, she asks each team to choose a "whistleblower." That person is given a toy whistle with directions to blow it whenever a team member begins to pass judgment on an idea. It's a fun but clear reminder of the importance of being open-minded. And in team situations, whistleblowing adds some wholesome competition as members notice if other teams are quiet or are getting whistled for being judgmental.

The whistleblower is rewarded with the whistle. The technique brings something new and different to a valuable activity — brainstorming — that too often is greeted with, "Oh no, not again."

Give trainees a "thumbs up" signal or the "okay" sign to thank, recognize, and encourage them, says Jodi Todd, customer service trainer for Microsoft in Redmond, WA.

The nonverbal cue lets participants know they're doing well or have asked a good question. It also shows she's focusing on them, and helps to enhance and maintain individuals' self-esteem.

Hand signals provide simple positive feedback

75

New theme gives ho-hum training shot in arm

A fresh theme and clever course titles can go a long way toward taking the edge off the "not another training program" attitude among employees, says Janell Manson, corporate training specialist at First Interstate Corp. of Wisconsin. She helps employees "get in shape" for changes in the bank structure and products with an internal marketing campaign titled "Sales Force Fitness."

The training program is set up in the same sequence as fitness program stages: Awareness, Initial Conditioning, Muscle Toning, Short-Term Sprinting, and The Marathon. Each stage represents a specific "shape up" program, beginning with the chairman, CEO, and president introducing the program (the Awareness stage) on video while working out in an exercise room, and ending with a lesson on becoming the best for the long run (The Marathon), presented by trainers wearing jogging shoes and other fitness attire during sessions.

Each training session is titled to fit the fitness theme. "Weight Loss Clinic" focused on the new "right-sized" organization chart and RPM is an acronym for the "revised product mix." And programs that are ongoing offerings are renamed to pique trainee interest. For example, the telephone and listening skills workshops are titled "Phonetastic Tips" and "Hear! Here!" respectively.

Manson says that not only have there been record numbers of employees attending internal training events, but she has also heard more off-the-cuff talk about training events, based on their titles alone.

76

Giving
long courses
a theme
makes
them more
palatable

Kathy Rodgers, manager of education for Southwestern Bell, Mission, KS, uses the yellow brick road from *The Wizard of Oz* to map progress in a multiweek, 71-lesson course for service representatives.

The yellow brick road graphically shows students their progress throughout the course, and also allows Rodgers to quickly see which lesson they're doing next. She prints each of the 71 topics on "yellow bricks" made of construction paper and tapes them in a path along a classroom wall that leads to the "Emerald City."

As each lesson is completed, a student puts a check mark on the appropriate brick. If students have questions on future lessons, Rodgers can easily and quickly look at the bricks and tell them at what point in the class their questions will be addressed.

She sometimes defers an answer until later in the course by having students post their questions on a "Question Tree." As their questions are answered, participants remove their Post-it Notes from the tree.

In her introductory remarks, Rodgers asks participants if they remember the story of Oz, and what Dorothy and her friends were looking for (to go back to Kansas, to gain a heart, courage, brain). At the close of the course, Rodgers gives participants graduation diplomas and tells them they now have the heart, courage, and knowledge to go out into the real world and succeed.

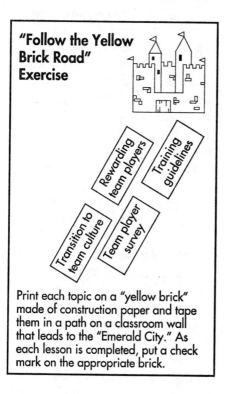

"Follow the Yellow Brick Road" Exercise

Rewarding team players

Training guidelines

Transition to team culture

Team player survey

Print each topic on a "yellow brick" made of construction paper and tape them in a path on a classroom wall that leads to the "Emerald City." As each lesson is completed, put a check mark on the appropriate brick.

Atypical training games spark trainees' energy levels

Participants in training at Great Plains Software in Fargo, ND, are told to arrive wearing a uniform and sneakers and to be prepared to "play ball."

Internal product trainer Jeanne Rodenbiker quickly converts her training room into a playing field, using chairs as bases, giving baseball hats to trainees, and keeping an inflatable bat on hand to add a little ballpark flavor. She divides the class into groups and has them choose their own names, usually something related to the course topic.

When the first team comes up to bat, one player draws a baseball card from a hat. Each card is marked as a single, double, triple, or home run. The pitcher (instructor) relays a question of the appropriate level of difficulty (for example, triples are more difficult than doubles). Although only one team member advances the bases, the entire team can discuss the question before answering. This eliminates putting students on the spot and encourages group interaction. If answers require visual aids, the team uses a whiteboard to diagram its responses.

The instructor serves as pitcher and umpire, providing hints or designating time limits as to when questions must be answered. After three outs (misses), the second team comes to bat.

Rodenbiker says the energy level in this exercise is usually high and teams become quite competitive. She has had teams develop cheers and a few enthusiastic players even slide into bases. In most courses, she fits in the game innings after completing major sections of the material.

78

Simple props demonstrate difficulties of phone conversations

Leehla Rutherford, a trainer with US West Direct, Aurora, CO, uses multicolored children's blocks to help trainees understand the difficulties involved in creating a "meeting of the minds" over the phone. She engages trainees in three activities to teach the importance of verbal and nonverbal communication, nuances of word meanings, creating word pictures, and abandoning preconceived ideas:

1. Two participants sit back-to-back. One participant constructs a design, while the other participant must attempt to reconstruct the design from a verbal description by the designer. They are allowed two minutes. The designs usually don't look at all alike.

2. Same time limit, two new participants. One builds a design and describes it as he completes it. The other participant cannot ask any questions until the two minutes are up. The second participant is then allowed to ask three questions. The result isn't perfect, but better than the first team's.

3. Two new participants, same time limit. Participants are allowed open conversation for the entire two minutes. Usually, Rutherford says, this team can construct two identical designs.

Teamwork goes on trial in a team-building exercise developed by Bonnie Murphy, new-business strategist for Hallmark Cards. She uses a "mock trial," with the prosecution "opposed" to teamwork and the defense "for" teamwork.

The group is divided into two teams, plus a judge and a bailiff. Each team selects two witnesses, a presenter to give an opening statement, another presenter to question witnesses, and a third presenter for a closing statement. Each team is allowed five minutes to present its case. Witnesses are not cross-examined, because it might make them feel defensive.

Murphy proceeds with the trial in the following order:

• Bailiff calls court to order and calls for all to stand for the judge.

• Opening statements by the prosecution and defense.

• The prosecution questions its own witnesses, as does the defense.

• Closing statements from the prosecution and defense.

• Closing statement and comments by the judge.

• Group evaluation of trial: What did they experience? How does it relate to their jobs or businesses? Additional comments and insights.

79

Putting teamwork 'on trial' accentuates its benefits

80

Trainee-created T-shirts make great review tools

To aid retention, Martha Longstreth, safety and training specialist for Hallmark Cards in Kansas City, MO, passes out plain white T-shirts and permanent marking pens or fabric pens to participants at the beginning of her courses. During breaks participants decorate the shirts with key words, thoughts, and ideas from the training.

Longstreth declares a "casual day" and everyone wears their T-shirts as reminders and encouragement for each other.

To show his trainees the importance of an open mind, creativity, and problem solving, Jack McKown, process controller for Hallmark Cards in Kansas City, MO, uses a "connect the dots" exercise as a brainteaser opener.

Draw a dot pattern (shown below) on a sheet of paper (make dots at least 1/4 inch diameter). Then ask participants to find how many straight lines they have to draw to connect all the dots. The only rule is that the lines must be drawn straight.

The purpose of the activity is to show participants that if they are creative, they can draw a line through all the dots by drawing only one line. After giving participants a few minutes, show them how to do the exercise (below).

Connect the Dots Exercise

To connect all the dots with one straight line, fold the paper over so all of the dots are touching, then connect the row of dots with a thick-line highlighter and unfold the paper.

82

Helping trainees dump work concerns frees their minds

Participants often are distracted by goings-on at work when they're in the classroom and can't be contacted, says Leon Noone, principal consultant with Training Australia in Turramurra. So Noone uses an exercise that not only acknowledges trainee concerns as genuine, but also helps them "dump" the concerns to enable them to concentrate on training.

Early in the session, Noone has participants list the things they're concerned about back at work — things they're afraid may "blow up" in their absence. He encourages participants to be specific and reassures them that their lists will be private.

He then hands out blank envelopes and asks participants to put their names on the envelopes and put their lists inside. Noone collects the envelopes and leaves them in a prominent place for the rest of the course,. He tells participants they may pick up their envelope at any time during the course and take any action they feel appropriate.

Noone says that once participants put their concerns on paper, they seem to stop worrying about them. They learn that the concern, while real to them, wasn't so important after all.

After identifying the course's "official objectives," Bob Norris, a trainer in Lake Worth, FL, asks the group to brainstorm this question: "If all your hopes for this course could come true, what would it do for your work group? Your organization? Yourself?" Norris posts the list on the wall and refers to it at the beginning of each day as "the target" for training.

"The exercise helps participants define to themselves the benefits of participating fully at the start," Norris says. "The training is in their terms, their context, which helps overcome resistance." Also, if training includes "visioning," the technique and its effectiveness are already demonstrated.

At the end of the course, Norris asks for an informal vote to see how close the group came to producing its desired training results.

83

Let trainees define for themselves benefits of participation

84

Give trainees incentive to change

Margaret Ashmore, a staff trainer with Houston Independent School District, illustrates the natural resistance to change — and how people often need motivation to initiate change — by putting a twist on a common exercise.

She asks participants to fold their arms across their chests in their usual manner, then asks them how it feels. They usually offer agreeable responses. Then she instructs them to unfold their arms and fold them again, but with the opposite arm on top. When asked how it feels, they now answer "strange" or "uncomfortable," Ashmore says.

She tells trainees research shows it takes at least 21 days to change a "minor" habit. They must allow themselves and others time to change, she says.

She goes a step further and says, "If I were to promise to give you $1,000 at the end of 21 days to fold your arms 'automatically' this new way, when would you start practicing?" Participants usually agree they would begin at once. From there, Ashmore goes into the benefits attendees will get from the session.

85

Action plans become reality when trainees stretch themselves

When Bob Schaumburg, senior trainer for US Sprint's Leadership Development group, Kansas City, MO, wants participants to understand the importance of "stretching" themselves and using all available resources in order to reach their personal — as well as the program's — objectives, he uses this exercise:

Before participants arrive for class, Schaumburg tapes strings (about five to seven inches in length for nine-foot ceilings) to blank index cards, then tapes the end of the string to the classroom ceiling so the cards hang down. After introductions, he instructs participants to stand under one of the cards and then do whatever is necessary to get the cards down.

"The tallest participants begin helping shorter ones when asked for assistance, and other attendees either reach, jump, or get chairs to stand on in order to pull the cards down," he says. Later, Schaumburg asks attendees to write a brief action plan on the card to take back to the job. The plans and the cards both serve as reminders for participants to stretch themselves, seek outside help, or go beyond their comfort zones to achieve their goals, he says.

86

Setting daily goals helps trainees stay focused

Setting goals each morning of a week-long training session is one way Anita Arney, branch training specialist at Stockton Savings Bank, Stockton, CA, motivates her participants. At the start of each day she briefly reviews upcoming information and then has each participant make a goal statement about the day's subject.

The goals are hung on a wall and at the end of each day Arney asks all participants if their goals have been achieved. At the end of the week, participants review their goal statements as groups. "Promoting ownership of goals facilitates their achievement and creates interaction among trainees," Arney says.

Examples of individual goals are:

• I will gain knowledge and understanding of all our products and services to enhance my customer service skills.

• I will use consistency and uniformity in everything from loan origination through loan closings.

Motivate your participants to reach for a better performance constantly with this technique used by Michelle Pickering, manager of food service, American Dairy Association, Okemos, MI. She asks three participants of varying heights to make a mark as far up as they can on a large sheet of paper posted on a wall. Then she asks each of them to try to surpass that mark with another reach. The second mark is invariably higher than the first, and Pickering makes the point that people can always achieve "a little bit more than they think they can."

87

Motivate trainees to reach for excellence constantly

88

Past participants' comments pique trainees' interest

Program success comes from prepared lessons, but also from prepared participants, says Hope Manruss, an instructional designer for Intel Corp., Chandler, AZ. She uses input from past attendees and managers to put course participants in a learning frame of mind.

She distributes a memo in advance to all participants and their managers that includes comments from previous graduates on the program's value.

Manruss asks the head of a division whose members are enrolled to start the first session by explaining how the training contributes to the division's strategic plan. Manruss requires participants *and* their managers to attend the meeting.

Next, a group of graduates talk about their experience in the program — their immediate reactions, their feelings during the program, and the long-term benefits they've seen.

He then has groups of managers and participants meet to brainstorm ways the program can be applied back on the job. The groups create a written learning contract and action plan. When class begins, trainees have a clear idea of what they will learn and how it will be of value.

Could you tell trainees the sky is green and get away with it? Robin Kilvert, a regional training manager with Mandarin Oriental, Hong Kong, forces trainees to question the trainer with this technique:

Begin the session by introducing the objectives and outlining them in the usual way. But instead of using the materials for the program you'll be offering, pass out materials for a first aid course (assuming that's not the course topic).

Continue your introduction to first aid until a confused participant interrupts to question your motives. When this happens make the point that if class members do not speak out when they have a question about the actual course topic a great deal will be lost to everyone in the group.

89

Throwing trainees a curve ball encourages them to question you

90

'Illustrate' the attributes of an ideal service provider

Participants work in teams to "illustrate" the attributes of the ideal service provider in customer service courses taught by Gerri Hura, director of training at Vista Host, Houston, TX. She suggests this exercise as a fun energizer and to facilitate team-building.

Hura conducts a five-minute brainstorming session with the group on the qualities of the "ideal" service provider. She posts responses on a flip-chart page. Examples include smiles, professional dress, good listening skills, etc.

She then breaks the group into smaller groups and assigns each group a part of the body: head, torso, and legs (for three groups) or head and body (two groups). She gives each group a flip-chart page and markers and tells them to work as a team to draw the head, torso, or legs of the ideal service provider, using the attributes they've described. She encourages them to create caricatures, accentuating body parts to illustrate characteristics. For example, big ears indicate a good listener or tennis shoes show the person is quick on their feet.

At the end of 10 minutes she has group members "autograph" their pictures and tape them to a classroom wall to make a complete body.

91

'Health break' reenergizes trainees

Instead of an afternoon coffee break, Lynne Bonnell, food and beverage manager at the Sheraton Centre Hotel, Toronto, Ontario, provides a "health break" during her sessions.

She leads attendees through a short series of low-impact aerobic exercises, such as toe-touchers, arm swings, and simple stretches. She often plays a videotape like Richard Simmons' *Sweating with the Oldies* to add to the fun. After the energizing workout, she serves juice, fruit, and yogurt instead of the usual coffee and rolls.

The intent of the health break, Bonnell says, is not to provide a true workout, but rather to reenergize students in an enjoyable way.

92

Let trainees provide positive feedback to each other

In addition to whatever positive feedback you are giving participants for energetic participation, insightful answers, and the like, allow them also to congratulate and compliment each other.

Kaye Stripling, assistant superintendent for a Houston independent school district, encourages participants to "give one another a hand." She has them draw an outline of their hand on a piece of paper and tape the outline to their backs. Throughout the day, people can write positive comments on the hand, and at day's end attendees remove the paper and read the comments.

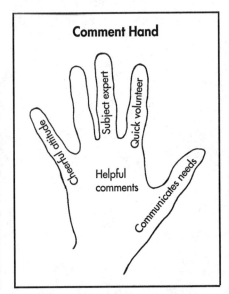

Comment Hand

Cheerful attitude

Subject expert

Quick volunteer

Helpful comments

Communicates needs

93

Trainees' experiences help reshape service strategies

Participants' own experiences with customer service can be used to revamp their respective company's service strategies. For example, Keith Taylor-Sharp, a vice president for Regis Corp., Minneapolis, uses a self-learning program called "What's Your Gripe?" where participants select an in-class panel to explore and evaluate the group's experience with customer service.

Group members ask questions of the panel about their gripes and concerns with various forms of service they have received — including experiences with their own companies. Root causes are examined for customer service problems such as being repeatedly transferred on the phone, long waits in line, or late deliveries. The group as a whole then explores possible solutions to those service problems.

Taylor-Sharp says the process empowers front-line workers to begin devising solutions to problems, taking them away from relying on upper management to make decisions that reshape customer service policies.

94

Reenacting news events offers trainees real-world lessons

All the classroom is a stage. At least in review sessions by Dan Finn, a regional training administrator for Nationwide Insurance, Visalia, CA.

At the conclusion of each segment, students bring news clippings related to course materials to class, and skits are designed around the stories. Participants are assigned roles to reenact the news events. Afterward, the group discusses practical points brought out by the drama.

For example, in a course on homeowners' insurance policies, a student might bring in a story of vandalism to property. Participants would play the roles of homeowner, police officer, contractor, and others. This would be followed by a discussion of what would be covered by various policies.

Holding an "information fair" allows participants access to diverse information in a short time.

Cyndy Martino, an educator with Baptist Medical Center in Jacksonville, FL, runs a one-day "risk management fair" each year to meet mandatory requirements on work safety. She sets up booths that feature information about a variety of safety issues. She uses puzzles, interactive exercises, demonstrations, subject matter experts (police, firefighters, etc.), computers, and videotapes to make training participatory and stimulating.

A booth on infection control, for instance, features handouts surreptitiously sprayed with Clue spray (available through security equipment supply houses) that later shows — under black light — every spot participants touch on their bodies. She also suggests offering participants rewards such as small prizes at some booths.

Martino says the fair saves her training department money because it combines several learning areas, cutting training time.

As a way to gauge learning, she tracks before- and after-training numbers of recurring incidents, such as infections and back injuries.

95

'Learning fair' combines several learning areas in one setting

96

Allow participants to explore their individual styles

To help make attendees conscious of how they present themselves, Gayle Waldron, a consultant with The Management Edge in Gainsville, FL, asks them to create unique name tents.

She gives participants 5 x 8 inch pieces of white poster board and a large supply of colored markers and crayons. She asks them to fold their pieces in half lengthwise, write their names at the top of one side and six adjectives or phrases that describe themselves on the back. The poster board is then folded into the form of a name tent, with participants' names on one side and adjectives on the back.

She says the exercise allows trainees to examine how they present themselves to others and their varying degrees of comfort with personal disclosure. At the end of the program, after trainees have learned about personality traits from an assessment instrument Waldron uses, they compare the assessment tool to their name/description tent characteristics. "It facilitates sharing personal information immediately and helps to validate the instrument," she says.

To help attendees see the positive aspects of conflict, Glenda Goodrich, a training specialist for Bear Creek Corp., Medford, OR, asks them to come up with a mnemonic device for "conflict," using single words or phrases. For example:

Challenge
Opportunity
Networking can result
Fixes a problem
Lessons will be learned
Improvement
Confidence is built
Thinking powers are stimulated

Because the exercise views conflict as positive, Goodrich says it can help attendees overcome resistance to conflict. All contributions are posted at the front of the room and discussed, creating individual and group reasons for handling conflict expediently and effectively.

97

Conflict: Not a burden, but an opportunity

98

Have trainees formulate questions before guest speakers arrive

Training sessions often include valuable presentations from outside subject-matter experts or senior managers from within the company. While those presentations may be full of information, director of training and development for The Vons Company Inc., Los Angeles, Wendy Kennedy says they often end without their full potential being tapped. Why? "The silence is usually deafening and awkward when the presenter says, 'Are there any questions?' It's not that participants don't have any questions; they're just afraid or ill-prepared to ask them."

Kennedy gets around that problem by telling participants — *before* the presentation begins — to write down questions that come to mind because each person will be individually asked if he or she has a question following the talk. The technique may put a little pressure on attendees, but Kennedy says it ultimately produces a round of high-quality questions and moves participants from a passive to active listening mode.

The key for trainers who use this technique, Kennedy says, is to make sure people know there is nothing wrong with *not* having a question.

To impress upon people the importance of coming to class with an open mind, Michael Chapman, a training officer for CSX Transportation, Jacksonville, FL, asks attendees to take a "training oath." He has them stand, raise their right hands, and say:

"I hereby agree in the presence of these, my friends and coworkers, and acknowledged by my uplifted hand that during this training session I will look for positive benefits of the material being taught regardless of what I may have seen or heard prior to coming to class. I further agree to have fun and participate in these proceedings to the best of my ability."

Chapman says asking attendees to "swear" to learning — and reminding them from time to time of the oath — goes a long way toward creating the buy-in necessary for any training program. He also reminds participants that they are the only people who can make the oath stick.

99

'Swearing in' trainees spurs them to participate

100

Collaboration triumphs over competition in 'nickel auction'

Lisa Schreiber, president of Novations in Omaha, NE uses this exercise to help participants explore alternatives to this common workplace problem: *lack of communication + uncertainty + perceived competition = irrational behavior.*

Called "nickel auction," the exercise requires 10 nickels, and starts with five chairs placed at the front of the classroom. Divide the large group into five smaller groups. Ask each group to pool their pocket change and give it to a group representative. Have those five reps come to the front of the room to sit with the other group reps.

In round one of the auction, ask each rep to bid or pass on one of the five nickels. Each nickel goes to the highest bidder, and bidding continues until all five nickels are gone. Send the reps back to their groups with the remaining change. Review which groups won bidding contests and how much they paid for each nickel (bidders have paid as much as $4 for a nickel).

Have groups pick new representatives for round two. But this time let the reps have a private discussion together for five minutes. They inevitably decide to each bid one cent for each nickel and allow everyone to get one.

Maxine McFarland, a senior technical writer with Roadnet Technologies Inc., Timmium, MD, uses this exercise to show that participants learn at different speeds depending on the subject, but given enough time, most everyone can master a skill.

She first discusses what being a slow, average, and fast learner means, then uses this short demonstration to determine which of those categories participants fall into: She asks each person to write the word "learner" with his or her left hand. When all are finished, she asks who had an easy time with the task, and who had a difficult time. Then she asks which of the participants had the advantage of being left-handed.

She then emphasizes again that learning speed is situational, and in this case the left-handers would be categorized as "fast" learners, whereas asked to write right-handed most left-handers might be lumped into the "slow" category.

101

Ability to master a skill isn't affected by learning speed

About the Author...

Robert Pike has been developing and implementing training programs for business, industry, government, and other professions since 1969. As president of Creative Training Techniques International Inc., Resources for Organizations Inc., and The Resources Group Inc., he leads more than 150 sessions each year on topics such as leadership, attitudes, motivation, communication, decision-making, problem-solving, personal and organizational effectiveness, conflict management, team-building, and managerial productivity.

More than 50,000 trainers have attended Pike's Creative Training Techniques workshops. As a consultant, he has worked with such organizations as American Express, Upjohn, Hallmark Cards Inc., IBM, PSE&G, Bally's Casino Resort, and Shell Oil. A member of the American Society for Training and Development (ASTD) since 1972, he has served on three of the organization's national design groups, and held office as director of special interest groups and as a member of the national board.

An outstanding speaker, Pike has been a presenter at regional and national conferences for ASTD and other organizations. He currently serves as co-chairman of the Professional Emphasis Groups for the National Speakers' Association. He was recently granted the professional designation of Certified Speaking Professional (CSP) by the NSA, an endorsement earned by only 170 of the organization's 3,800 members.

Pike is editor of Lakewood Publications' *Creative Training Techniques Newsletter*, author of *The Creative Training Techniques Handbook*, and has contributed articles to *TRAINING Magazine*, *The Personnel Administrator*, and *Self-Development Journal*. He has been listed, since 1980, in *Who's Who in the Midwest* and is listed in *Who's Who in Finance and Industry*.

Want More Copies?

This and most other Lakewood books are available at special quantity discounts when purchased in bulk. For details write Lakewood Books, 50 South Ninth Street, Minneapolis, MN 55402. Call (800) 707-7769 or (612) 333-0471. Or fax (612) 340-4819. Visit our web page at www.lakewoodpub.com.

More on Training

Powerful Audiovisual Techniques: 101 Ideas to Increase the Impact and Effectiveness of Your Training $14.95

Dynamic Openers & Energizers: 101 Tips and Tactics for Enlivening Your Training Classroom $14.95

Optimizing Training Transfer: 101 Techniques for Improving Training Retention and Application $14.95

Managing the Front-End of Training: 101 Ways to Analyze Training Needs — And Get Results! $14.95

Motivating Your Trainees: 101 Proven Ways to Get Them to Really Want to Learn $14.95

Creative Training Techniques Handbook: Tips, Tactics, and How-To's for Delivering Effective Training, 2nd Edition $49.95

Creative Training Techniques Newsletter: Tips, Tactics, and How-To's for Delivering Effective Training $ 99/12 issues